60 Hot To Touch Accessible Web Design Tips – the tips no web developer can live without!

Jim Byrne

Thanks

Thanks for purchasing '60 Hot To Touch Accessible Web Design Tips – the tips no web developer can live without'.

For 4 years I produced a fortnightly accessible web design tip and sent it off to my mailing list of interested subscribers. These are the best of the bunch. I hope you find them useful in your web design work.

I would like to thank all the talented web developers who have supplied me with 'juicy' tips through their articles and emails. They have encouraged me to keep learning about the endlessly fascinating job of creating accessible sites. Particular thanks goes to Gez Lemon, Mel Pedley, Rich Pedley and Mike Pepper for inspiration and technical review of these tips.

Don't hesitate to get in touch with your comments or suggestions about how I can improve future editions of this book. Email me at webdesign@jimbyrne.co.uk. I look forward to hearing from you.

Visit my website at http://www.jimbyrne.co.uk to find more ebooks, articles, training courses and services related to Accessible Web Design.

Special thanks goes to my wife Pat for her unconditional love and encouragement.

All the best,

Jim.

Cover design by Sue Irving of Open Creative.

PUBLISHER INFORMATION

60 Hot To Touch Accessible Web Design Tips – the tips no web developer can live without!

Copyright © 2006 Jim Byrne

ISBN 978-1-4116-6729-7

Contents

About Jim Byrne

Jim has been programming computers and involved in the technical issues of computing since the late 1970s. He has been promoting the benefits of accessible web practices since 1996, when he founded the not-for-profit accessible web design consultancy 'The Making Connections Unit' with his colleague David Donald.

He has written and spoken widely on the subject of accessible Web design, including on national radio and television.

In the early 1990s he worked as a Disability Information Officer and Trainer with The Wellbeing Initiative, a training organisation set up to help disabled people get back into work. This raised his awareness of equality and access issues, and he became interested in finding ways to remove the barriers disabled people face when trying to access information and services.

In 2001 he was identified as one of the 'movers and shakers in e-commerce in Scotland' for his work in the area of web accessibility (NB Magazine, June, 2001).

Jim is the founder and a proud member of the worldwide Guild of Accessible Web Designers – an association of organisations and accessible web developers: http://www.gawds.org

Other publications

Accessible Web Typography, an introduction for web designers published by ScotConnect ISBN: 0-9545375-1-3
http://www.scotconnect.com/webtypography/webtypebook.php

Creating Accessible PDFs with Adobe Acrobat 6, published by ScotConnect ISBN: 0-9545375-1-4
http://www.scotconnect.com/pdfs/accesspdfs.php

Standards for Disability Information and Advice Provision in Scotland: Making Websites Accessible (November 2002), published by The Scottish Accessible Information Forum. ISBN 0-9543408-0-9

Towards a Communications and Information Technology Intensive Learning Environment: Supplementing a Political Economy Module: (2000) David Donald, Alan Hutton and Jim Byrne in Innovative Approaches to Learning and Teaching in Economics and Business Higher Education. Stafford University Press ISBN 1897898 82 7

Developer of a number of Web applications including:

QnECMS (Quick 'n' Easy Content Management System) - the accessible content management system http://www.qnecms.co.uk. A feature rich content management system suitable for individuals, businesses and colleges.

Extracurricular activities

Photography - see Jim's West End Photo Diary at http://www.glasgowwestend.co.uk/gallery/.

Writing songs and playing rock guitar in the band Loris.

Assisting his wife Pat run 'Pat's Guide to the West End of Glasgow: http://www.glasgowwestend.co.uk/

Accessible web design is not about creating boring sites

Accessible websites can look fabulous, be interactive and use up-to-date multimedia capabilities (for example, images, sound, movies, Javascript, photographs and server-side technologies like PHP or ASP).

You can use all the 'stuff' you deem appropriate to your audience and message, have a site that is accessible and passes 'Bobby' or other accessibility checks.

What is required when using these technologies is a bit of clear thinking about what their purpose is on your site, and how, if the content is important, their functionality or message can be provided in alternative ways.

For example, provide alt attributes and title tags for your images and photographs. Ensure that your site still functions on Web browsers that don't support Javascript and provide captions or transcripts of movies and sound.

Admittedly it is not always easy: for example, captioning of multimedia is a difficult skill to master. However, most accessibility techniques are not 'rocket science'. They will actually add to the 'richness' of the experience for your visitors.

Accessible websites can still be great looking websites. For proof, check the entries in the 'Site of the Month' competition run by the Guild of Accessible Web Designers at http://www.gawds.org.

Links

CSS Zen Garden: http://www.csszengarden.com/

2.

Test the accessibility of your web page with your own web browser

Almost all web browsers allow you to change the text size, font, colour and background colour of the web pages you visit.

Use this functionality to check how your pages look with much larger or smaller text, or a different text/background combination. Check if the page design allows these attributes to be altered at all.

If they can't be altered (perhaps because you have spent time trying to force the page to look the same on everybody's screen), then this should alert you to the fact that your pages may not be as accessible as you thought.

An important aspect of accessible web design is giving users the ability to change the presentation of the page to suit their own needs - if they can't do that then it should alert you to accessibility issues with your site.

You can find out more about how to change browser preferences on Lois Wakeman's excellent website at http://lois.co.uk/services/access.shtml.

Update to tip 2: You can now install additional toolbars on both Internet Explorer and Firefox to test the accessibility of your website. See the article 'Evaluating Web Sites for Accessibility with Firefox' by Patrick H. Lauke: http://www.gawds.org/show.php?contentid=150

3.

Use relative units when setting CSS text sizes

Using relative units when setting CSS text sizes will make your web pages accessible to a wider audience.

There is no one 'perfect size' for text on the web; different people prefer different sizes. Personally, I prefer the text on web pages to be quite big, so that I don't have to squint to read it. With this in mind I have set the text size preference in my web browser a few points larger than the default.

However, I still come across text on web pages that is too small for me to read, e.g., there are pages that ignore the preferences that I have set in my browser. The designer has tried to control the text size I see on my screen, making it less accessible. That usually means they have used an absolute unit of measurement, such as points or inches, when setting the size of text on the page.

To ensure that the user of your web pages can set the size of text to suit their own preferences you should control text sizes with relative units in a Cascading Style Sheet (CSS)or not set a text size at all. Relative units are em units, percentages and relative keywords such as smaller or bigger.

More detailed information about this can be found in my book 'Accessible Web Typography, an introduction for web designers' which you will find on the web at http://www.scotconnect.com/webtypography/webtypebook.php

Don't rely on colour alone to provide important information

When creating a web form, don't write, 'the fields with a red dot next to them are compulsory, those with a green dot are optional.' This statement will be of no use to people who are colour blind, and to those using grey-scale monitors or screen readers.

Requiring users to differentiate between colours to access important information can lead to problems. An example would be a navigation button that has red text on a green background, as people who have difficulty differentiating between red and green (the most common kind of colour blindness) will have a hard time trying to navigate the site.

The main colour combinations to avoid for people who are colour blind:

Red/green combinations (memory aid: red berries against green leaves on a tree)

Blue/yellow combinations (memory aid: yellow daffodils against a blue sky)

'The Institute for Dynamic Educational Advancement (IDEA) and Brandeis University' provide some useful information about colour blindness at http://webexhibits.org/causesofcolor/2.html

Links

The Institute for Dynamic Educational Advancement (IDEA): http://webexhibits.org/causesofcolor/2.html

5.

Ensure links work when Javascript doesn't

If you use Javascript to 'jazz up' the navigation on your website, make sure the links still work when Javascript is turned off. A technique I have often seen used on web pages involves Javascript being used to open a new window when a user clicks a link:

```
<a href="javascript:
popwin("/contact_us/default.htm")">Contact
Us</a>
```

Note that in the above example the URL of the page being linked to will only appear as a result of running the script. This is not good, as a user who has Javascript turned off or not available will not be able to link to this particular page.

You can be sure that whatever you are trying to achieve with your Javascript, there will be a more accessible way to do it and that is true in this case. The following example is from Evolt.org, and shows how the same effect can be achieved without breaking the link:

```
<a href="/contact_us/default.htm"
target="newWindow"
onclick="window.open(this.href, this.target);
return false">Contact Us</a>
```

Please note: the W3C guidelines say that you should always warn users before opening a new window.

Links

Evolt.org Javascript article: http://www.evolt.org

Link text should describe the content linked to

This tip is a very short one. Ensure that the text used for links adequately describes the page or content being linked to. Link text should be short and descriptive and ideally still make sense when read out of context.

Some people using screen readers will be navigating through your site by jumping from link to link; if all your links say 'click here' the usability and accessibility of your site is considerably reduced.

7.

Accessibility is not enough

Jakob Neilson, the usability expert, believes that the current focus on accessibility techniques isn't covering all bases. He says, 'to help these users accomplish critical tasks, you must adopt a usability perspective'.

Focussing on good usability practice is essential to making websites that are both accessible and easy to use.

In November 2005, user experience consultancy User Vision surveyed 208 disabled users throughout the UK and asked them to rank in order of preference their most important issues when browsing websites. The results were surprising in that they did not focus on access issues, but instead on more general usability issues:

- Clear content, straightforward language and a clear, simple layout.

- Good navigation and the ability to know where you are within a site.

- Meaningful and clear hyperlinks.

Links

Disabled web users rank their usability priorities: http://www.out-law.com/default.aspx?page=6314

Accessibility Is Not Enough:
http://www.useit.com/alertbox/accessibility.html

8.

Introduce yourself to the Web Content Accessibility Guidelines

The Web Content Accessibility Guidelines and associated documents published by the The World Wide Web Consortium (W3C) are a fantastic resource and are recognised as the 'standard' reference documents for those building accessible sites. However, they can be difficult for the beginner to understand and can seem rather overwhelming in the breadth of issues they cover.

In this tip, I suggest an alternative 'entry point' to learning the guidelines; the 'WAI Web Content Accessibility Curriculum' website created by Chuck Letourneau and Geoff Freed at http://www.w3.org/WAI/wcag-curric/overgid.htm

On the above site you will find lots of examples and explanations for each checkpoint - plenty of help to get you started.

Links

WAI Web Content Accessibility Curriculum:
http://www.w3.org/WAI/wcag-curric/overgid.htm

Add a full stop to the end of alt attributes and list items

When creating text for your alt attributes always add a full stop at the end of the text. This will help people who are using screen-reading software to differentiate the image label from any surrounding text.

It is also a good idea to add a full stop at the end of each item in a list, helping to make the distinction between each item clearer for those who do not have any visual clues.

Make PDFs more accessible

The joy of the web is that you can deliver all sorts of different media via a single interface. Tim Berners-Lee designed it with exactly that in mind.

That is good news in terms of accessibility, because it means you can offer the same content in a choice of formats, for example, you could provide a PDF version for printing, or a photograph to help reinforce an idea.

The current version of Adobe PDF has many accessibility features that previous versions lacked:

- Text can now be read by a selection of screen readers.

- There is support for high contrast viewing.

- Structured markup can be added to PDF documents (just like HTML) - making it easier for those using screen readers to navigate.

When creating PDFs always use the most up-to-date version, and the new features developed by Adobe, to ensure your documents are accessible to the widest possible audience.

Unfortunately, despite recent improvements in the accessibility features, it is still quite difficult to create fully accessible PDF documents. For the best result, use all the techniques available, then employ suitable users to test your documents.

Note: HTML is a more accessible format than PDF; I am not suggesting you use PDF as your default way of delivering documents on the web.

Links

How to Create Accessible PDFs with Adobe Acrobat 6, by Jim Byrne:
http://www.jimbyrne.co.uk/show.php?contentid=54

Adobe – How to create accessible Adobe Acrobat files:
http://www.adobe.com/products/acrobat/access_booklet.html

 **11.**

Add alt attributes to spacer and decorative images

Always add an empty alt attribute to every spacer or decorative image you use in your website, for example, `<img src="spacer.gif" alt="">`.

If spacer or decorative images have no alt attributes, then people browsing with images off, or with text browsers, will either see or hear the file name or the text '[image]' for each image lacking an alt attribute.

As spacer images tend to be liberally sprinkled throughout many websites, having to listen to the words '[image]' 150 times on each page of a site can be very annoying.

Using valid markup and style sheets for presentation should help you dispense with the need for spacer images on your site and consequently you will spend less time adding empty alt attributes to images.

12. Make forms easier to use by creating a logical tab order

The only time I use a keyboard when browsing the web is when I am filling in a form. In common with many other keyboard users (for example, web surfers who are blind) I use the tab key to move from one field to the next. So I tend to notice when the order in which I cycle through the fields does not seem logical or sensible.

If not specifically set by the designer, the order in which the tab key takes me through a form is determined by the order the fields appear in the HTML code.

Most of the time this is ok, but because many designers design the layout of forms using tables, occasionally there is an inconsistency between the visual order of input fields and the order that they appear in the HTML. These inconsistencies will lower the usability of a site, as the 'route' taken through the form will seem erratic and potentially confusing.

You can use the taborder attribute to specifically set the 'order-of-travel' through your forms.

This is an easy technique to master: each taborder attribute is assigned a number - the 'order-of-travel' is from lowest number to highest:

```
Name : <input type = "text" name =
"membername" tabindex="1">

Email: <input type = "text" name = "email"
tabindex="2">
```

13. Give visitors your content first (not your navigation)

Does your website use a table or CSS to place the navigation bar on the left hand side, and main content on the right?

If so, it is no bad thing: visitors will instantly understand this design convention and won't have to waste time trying to figure out how to get around your site.

However, there is a problem with this 'standard layout' for people using screen readers. Accessing a website using a screen reader is a 'linear process': the text that comes first gets read first. If the navigation is the first thing on the page that is what gets read first.

If your navigation bar contains a lot of links, that can mean a lot of wasted time before a screen reader user gets the content of your page.

I was recently reminded of a very elegant 'table hack' , while reading 'Building Accessible Websites' by Joe Clark http://www.joeclark.org/, that can help users get around this problem. Instead of coding your table in the conventional manner as in the example below:

```
<table>
<tr>
<td>Navigation menu</td>
<td>Page Content</td>
</tr>
</table>
```

you can use the following rather elegant 'hack' to ensure the content on your page is presented first, and the navigation second:

```
<table>
```

```
<tr>
<td>(put a single pixel gif here)</td>
<td rowspan="2">Page Content</td>
</tr>
<tr>
<td>The navigation menu goes here.</td>
</tr>
</table>
```

As you can see, it uses an 'empty' table cell in the first row which is directly above the navigation bar, and then the content cell is in the right hand cell (the content cell spans both rows).

There are many techniques you can use to help visitors get straight to your valuable content, including providing a 'skip to content' link before the start of your left hand navigation. Joe Clark covers many useful techniques in his book 'Building Accessible Websites' free on the web at http://joeclark.org/book/sashay/serialization/Chapter08.html

Links

A Promotion Guide: http://www.apromotionguide.com/tabletrick.html

Building Accessible Websites by Joe Clark: http://joeclark.org/book/sashay/serialization/Chapter08.html

14.

Design for machines first, people second!

No web page has ever been created that can be transmitted directly to the brain without first being mediated through some type of hardware and software (e.g. a computer and a web browser). The best chance you have of your web page being accessible to this 'intermediate layer' is to create your pages using standards-based markup (e.g., XHTML).

Visitors won't be able to access your content if your pages don't work on the browser they are using - be it a refreshable braille reader, a WebTV, or the latest PC running Internet Explorer 6. The secret to success is to 'code to standards'.

If you code to standards (for example, HTML 4.01 or XHTML 1), you have the best chance of your web page working on the 'dumb' machines that know nothing other than 'how to follow the rules'. This allows them to render the structure of a page to an output device. It doesn't guarantee your content will be accessible to everyone, but if you follow the rules, you will already be well down the road towards building an accessible website.

Links

Web page validation tools: http://www.htmlhelp.com/tools/validator/

Cynthia Says web accessibility checker: http://www.contentquality.com/

15.

Provide additional keyboard access to your web pages

Accesskey is an attribute that can be added to an element (for example, a form field) so that a user can jump to that element by using a keyboard command. Pressing the appropriate combination of keys, 'gives focus' to the associated element, for example, if used in a form, the cursor jumps to the form input field.

Here is an example of adding the accesskey attribute to the label of a form field. As the label is associated with an input element, the input element gets focus, that is, the cursor jumps to that form field:

```
<label for="name" accesskey="1">Name
(accesskey 1): </label>
<input type = "text" name = "membername"
id="name">
```

The accesskey attribute can be added to the following elements: a, input, textarea, button, label, area, label, and legend. The behaviour of the accesskey attribute depends on the type of element it is assigned to: for instance, on a form field it give 'focus' to the field but for links it means the user jumps to the page being linked to.

The keys that a user needs to press will depend on the operating system and browser being used. In general, the accesskey can be invoked on the Windows platform by pressing the 'Alt key' and the access key character, and on the Mac by pressing the 'Ctrl key' and the accesskey character.

There are problems with accesskey you should be aware of. For instance, 'how will the user know what keyboard shortcuts to use for the various elements on the webpage?'

The UK government makes an attempt to get around this problem by publishing a list of recommended accesskeys: http://www.e-envoy.gov.uk/oee/oee.nsf/sections/webguidelines-content/$file/04.htm#4

Visit the 'WATS.ca' site for further information, and a discussion on the downsides of using the accesskey attribute.

Links

WATS.ca: http://wats.ca/resources/accesskeys/19

UK government Access Key recommendations: http://www.e-envoy.gov.uk/oee/oee.nsf/sections/webguidelines-content/$file/04.htm#4

16.

Expand your abbreviations and acronyms

If your web pages are littered with acronyms and abbreviations (for example, HTML, W3C, CSS), you will be pleased to know that HTML 4 (and above) provides a way to expand those abbreviations without clogging up your pages with additional text.

What is the difference between an abbreviation and an acronym?

Abbreviations are any shortened form of written words that represent the complete form, such as UK for United Kingdom, MCU for Making Connections Unit, or etc for etcetera.

Acronyms are abbreviations that are used as a word in their own right when read aloud, such as RADAR or NASA.

Here is an example of how to use the <abbr> element in your web page:

```
<p>Use standard <abbr title="HyperText Markup
Language">HTML</abbr> to markup and <abbr
title="Cascading Style Sheets">CSS</abbr> for
presentation.</p>
```

When the user hovers their mouse over the abbreviation, a 'tool tip' will appear containing the expanded form.

Unfortunately, Internet Explorer on Windows does not support the <abbr> element. However, there are a number of ways to overcome this, the simplest one being that suggested by Marek Prokop:

Create the following declaration in your style sheet:

```
abbr, acronym, span.abbr { cursor: help;
border-bottom: 1px dashed #000; }
```

Add an additional <span> element when using the <abbr> element:

```
<abbr title="HyperText Markup Language"><span
class="abbr" title="Cascading Style
Sheets">HTML</span></abbr>
```

If this seems too much like hard work Marek also provides a way to automate this 'workaround' http://www.sovavsiti.cz/css/abbr.html.

I tend to given and explanation of an acronym or abbreviation when it first appears – for example, XHTML (Extensible Hypertext Markup Language) and use the abbreviation thereafter. Dependent on copy length, I make a judgement call and may introduce another instance of the tag(s). Overdoing it can become repetitive verbiage.

Links

Styling <abbr> in IE by Marek Prokop:
http://www.sovavsiti.cz/css/abbr.html

17.

Make a start on those 'legacy' pages

This tip is short, and not technical. It is aimed at organisations who have a huge number of inaccessible legacy web pages and want to find a way to get started down the road to making them accessible. How do you start without it feeling like a frightening and overwhelming task?

One way to get started is to prioritise your pages according to their popularity with your visitors, then begin by making the most popular pages of your website(s) accessible first.

This assumes that you have access to visitor statistics for your website. If not, then your first task is to put in place a way to gather statistics for your site(s).

Having made a start, you can then plan to ensure that all of your pages are made accessible - including those you are creating today.

18.

Sort your 'character encoding'

If you have used the World Wide Web Consortium (W3C) HTML Validator (http://validator.w3.org/), you will have noticed that it requires information about character encoding before it will check your pages. What does 'character encoding' mean, and what encoding should you use?

It is a complicated subject; however, the following simplification should give you the basic idea.

A character encoding is a particular match up between a set of numbers and a set of characters, for example, the character encoding called US ASCII (international standard ISO 646) consists of 256 numbers and each of these numbers represents a character, (letters from the alphabet, numbers, or some other character). For example, 65 represents A, 66 is B and so on.

Not all languages use the Western Alphabet, so there are encodings that will match the numbers up with different characters (for example, Japanese characters). The browser on your local computer checks to see what character encoding you are using so that it can display the page appropriately.

For example, if you have indicated that you are using 'ISO 646', the browser knows that this is US ASCII so it will display the page using English characters.

Links

List of common character sets: http://www.w3.org/International/O-charset-lang.html

19.

How do you add character encoding information to a web page?

For HTML 4.01, you can indicate the character encoding in the head of your page using the following meta tag:

```
<meta http-equiv="Content-Type" content="text/html; charset=iso-8859-1">
```

ISO-8859-1 (commonly called Latin 1) is the default characters set for HTTP 1.1 and indicates a set of common English characters. Generally, this is the most common character set indicated in web pages and is likely to be the one you will use.

Creating valid HTML is one of the most important steps you can take when designing accessible websites. If you do not provide the appropriate character encoding, this could lead to characters in your page not displaying correctly, which will have an impact on the accessibility of your content.

Links

W3C: HTML Document Representation:
http://www.w3.org/TR/html401/charset.html

20.

Don't try to control visitors to your site

There is nothing more irritating to users than a site that appears to be trying to control them, either by forcing them down particular paths or by disabling features of the browser interface.

Examples of trying to control visitors include:

- Opening new windows, so that the original site is still hovering in the background. If users want to come back to your site they can click the back button, and if they want to open a new window they can do it themselves.

- Using scripts to disable the back button, disable right clicking, or subvert some other aspect of the browser interface.

These techniques can decrease accessibility as they go against user expectations about how the web works. I expect to be able to click the back button in my browser to move back to the last page I viewed, or leave a site altogether.

Undermining such conventions can be particularly confusing for the 'non-visual' user, who may expect a particular sequence of events to happen and become confused when events don't happen in the anticipated way.

21.

Add structural meaning to image-based headings

Cascading Style Sheets allow a certain degree of control over font choice, line height, font size and so on. For many designers this limited control is still not enough and they continue to use images instead of text for their web page headlines.

Here is a tip for adding some structural meaning to those image-based headings - a technique first suggested to me by Patrick H. Lauke.

When using a graphic as a heading, enclose the image tag in the appropriate structural markup:

```
<h1><img src="mculogo.jpg" height="48"
width="171" alt="The Making Connections
Unit"></h1>
```

For users of screen readers such as Jaws, the text in the alt attribute will be recognised as a heading, thus retaining its structural meaning.

Decide whether your non-text elements are functional, decorative or providing content

Labels should be added to all non-text content; the alt attribute is a requirement for both HTML 4 and XHTML W3C standards-based documents.

When trying to decide on the text label required for particular non-text elements, I find it helps to think of them as falling roughly into one of three categories: functional, decorative (including layout) or providing content.

Functional

For functional images, including navigation bars, the text should describe the function or destination. For example, if an image is used as a search button, the alt attribute could be 'Search'. If an image is used for navigation, the alt attribute should describe the destination. Usually the alt attribute for functional images contains the same text as appears on the graphic button or navigation bar.

Providing content

For images that contain important content, the alt attribute should provide a short description of the content (a few words that sum up the content). Use the title or longdesc attributes for longer descriptions.

Decorative including layout images

For purely decorative images, or images used to help with the layout of a page, the alt attribute should be empty (alt="").

23.

How to make printable characters between adjacent links invisible

Some older screen readers are unable to distinguish between adjacent links if there is no printable character between them. The W3C Web Content Accessibility Guidelines 1.0 provide a priority 3 checkpoint to deal with this unfortunate behaviour of older screen readers:

10.5 Until user agents (including assistive technologies) render adjacent links distinctly, include non-link, printable characters (surrounded by spaces) between adjacent links.

The obvious place where you can find several adjacent links is on a horizontal navigation bar at the top or bottom of a web page. So how do you adhere to this guideline in situations where displaying a printed character in your navigation bar would upset your beautifully crafted design?

This tip shows a technique I have used on the Glasgow West End website http://www.glasgowwestend.co.uk. The printable characters separating links are rendered invisible by making them the same colour as the navigation bar background:

```
<a href="/postcards.php">postcards</a>
<span style="color: #000000;">|</span>
<a href="/classified.php">classified ads</a>
```

In this particular instance I have used a vertical bar to separate adjacent links, and the background for the navigation bar is black. I have used inline style information to set the colour attribute of the vertical bar to black - thus rendering it invisible. Best practice is to avoid using inline styles and use external style sheets to set your presentation preferences.

In response to this tip, Mike Pepper of the web design company, 'Enigma' suggested an alternative technique to hide printable characters: set the style for the vertical bar to display: none. As Mike says, 'It is a lot simpler and it deals with the content/form issue'.

Links

W3C WCAG Checkpoint 10.5: http://www.w3.org/TR/WCAG10/#gl-interim-accessibility

Mike Pepper: http://www.seowebsitepromotion.com/

Use absolute-size keywords to set the text size on your pages

Although I am on record as advocating the use of em units as the best way of setting text sizes on web pages, an alternative unit of measurement has recently worked its way into my consciousness: 'absolute-size keywords'.

Despite the name, absolute-size keywords are actually a relative measurement: text size is calculated relative to the default font size set in the user's browser. The idea is that they replace the sizes previously provided by the font tag. The following absolute-size keywords are available for your style sheet:

xx-small

x-small

small

medium

large

x-large

xx-large

Why absolute size keywords are a good idea

There are at least four very good reasons for adopting absolute-size keywords as your relative unit of choice.

Absolute-size keywords are a relative unit of measurement, allowing users to resize text to suit their own needs.

The size of absolute-size keywords will be based on the default size set in the users browser. If users have set a font size that they are comfortable with, their preferences will not be undermined by the use of absolute size keywords in your webpage design.

Absolute-size keywords do not suffer from the 'inheritance' problems related to using em units, percentages, and the relative keywords of bigger and smaller. When changing font size using standard browser preferences (for example, not zoom) the text does not become unreadably small or unusably large (in standards-compliant browsers. A keyword used to set the size of a paragraph does not inherit the value of a keyword set in the body element or any other parent element.

Small is always small, xx-small is always xx-small. In the most up-to-date Internet Explorer browsers, xx-small (the smallest size) will never be smaller than 9pt, which is the readability threshold on a Mac.

Unfortunately, there are some problems with absolute-size keywords, mostly due to the inconsistent browser support (see tip number 54 for a suggested solution). Techniques have been developed that can help you get around most of the problems. The most useful 'workarounds' are summarised in my free e-book, 'Accessible Web Typography, an introduction for web designers' at http://www.jimbyrne.co.uk/show.php?contentid=54

Links

Accessible Web Typography, an introduction for web designers: http://www.jimbyrne.co.uk/show.php?contentid=54

25.

Use favelets to check validation and accessibility of your web pages

Favelets provide you with a way to run short scripts embedded within bookmarked URLs. The script will act on the page you currently have in your browser. Scripts are invoked by choosing the bookmark from your bookmark or favourites menu. This is a powerful feature that you can put to good use when creating and validating your web pages.

You can use favelets for many things, including:

- Validating HTML and CSS.

- Resetting browser screen size (for example, for checking how a page will look on screens with a different resolutions).

- Displaying images on a page with their alt attributes.

Ian Lloyd has a good explanation of how to use favelets on his 'Accessibility-checking favelets' page at http://www.accessify.com/tools-and-wizards/accessibility-checking-favelets.asp.

His tutorial is aimed at Windows users. If you are a Mac user or using another platform, I am confident you will be able to work out how to use them from his explanation.

Links

More useful favelets related to accessibility and validation can be found at:

Tantek Çelik list of favelets: http://tantek.com/favelets/

Structure your menus by marking them up as lists

A navigation menu is, speaking structurally, a list; but it is rare to find a developer/designer who marks them up as such.

I guess the reason for this is that designers don't want to have big ugly bullet points littering their menus, or seemingly uncontrollable margins throwing out their carefully crafted layouts.

Is it possible to use the correct structural markup and still make your menus look the way you want them to?

A recent rash of articles and tools has appeared to demonstrate that the answer is a resounding yes. You can use CSS to style lists to look more or less any way you want.

First, undermine your previous assumptions by visiting the 'Listamatic' website to see examples of different list styles (with the CSS used for each): http://www.maxdesign.com.au/presentation/listamatic/.

Then visit Mark Newhouse's Taming Lists tutorial to learn how to make your own. http://www.alistapart.com/stories/taminglists/.

And finally - if you can't be bothered learning how to do it yourself - have a look at Accessify's new List-o-matic - where you fill in a few forms, and the List-o-matic tool does all the hard work for you http://www.accessify.com/tools-and-wizards/list-o-matic/list-o-matic.asp .

Why is this relevant to accessible web design?

Using the appropriate markup for all the structures in your web documents is the first step towards making them accessible. Web pages need to be accessible to the tools, for example, the 'user agents' people use first, before they can be accessible to the people themselves. Using valid standards-based markup means you have the best chance of your pages being understood by those intermediate 'user agents' - that usually means computers and web browsers to you and me.

Links

Listamatic: http://www.maxdesign.com.au/presentation/listamatic/

A List Apart – taming lists:
http://www.alistapart.com/stories/taminglists/

Accessify List-o-matic: http://www.accessify.com/tools-and-wizards/list-o-matic/list-o-matic.asp

27.

Use HTML attributes or CSS to set web page colours, but don't use both

Here is a useful tip that I found while browsing the Accessibility Internet Rally 2003 Advanced Training website.

Use HTML attributes or CSS to set web page colors, but don't use both.

For example, if you set the background colour in a table cell to black using an HTML attribute (for instance, bgcolor="#000000") and used CSS to create contrasting white text (style ="color: #FFFFFF") you will start getting emails from users who surf with style sheets off or those using browsers that don't support style sheets.

I haven't come across anyone yet who can read black text on a black background.

Links

Accessibility Internet Rally 2003 Advanced Training website:
http://www.cookiecrook.com/AIR/2003/train/title.php

28.

If you need help, ask an expert!

Where do you go when you have a question related to accessible web design? If you are like me, you probably spend too much time searching for and then browsing through the many good accessible web design websites. You probably hope that one of them will have the answer to your current question.

Search no more. If you need help, ask an expert. You can do that by visiting a discussion forum which is populated by some of the web's most knowledgeable accessible web design experts. It is called AccessifyForum.com and it has been set up by Nigel Peck of MIS Web Design and Ian Lloyd of Accessify.com.

The forum is already a busy 'junction' for experts and beginners alike. So don't sit on that question a minute longer – ask and you shall receive.

Links

Accessify Forum: http://www.accessifyforum.com/index.php

29.

Understanding colour contrast and accessibility

In terms of accessibility colour is one of the areas I find hardest to understand. I can read a sentence such as:

'avoid using colors of similar lightness adjacent to one another, even if they differ in saturation or hue.' (Taken from http://www.lighthouse.org/color_contrast.htm)

And be as confused after I've read it as I was before.

I guess that is because I've not done a course on colour theory and I'm thrown by the jargon. In this tip I will define the words hue, lightness and saturation. Having figured out what they mean, I can try to explain the above advice. Bear in mind that with these definitions I am simplifying as much as I can.

Hue:

This is the easy one - just substitute the word 'colour' for the word hue and you have the meaning.

Lightness:

How much light does the colour reflect? Black doesn't reflect much, white reflects lots. Colours thus appear light or dark; how light or dark they are tells you their 'lightness'.

Saturation:

The purity of the colour - saturated colours contain no white, grey, black or complementary colours.

So now I'll put the advice from the Lighthouse website into words I understand:

Even when using different colours next to one another (for example, text and a background colour), if they are similarly light or similarly dark there will still be accessibility issues for some users.

Phew, perhaps this 'colour business' is not as impenetrable as I thought!

Links

The Theory of Colour: definitions:
http://paintcafe.sympatico.ca/en/couleur/langage/vocabulaire/

Lighthouse International: http://www.lighthouse.org/index.html

30.

Use alternative style sheets to give users control of critical elements such as text size or colour

I apologise if this tip is a bit more 'techy' than usual. It just happens to be about a topic I was particularly interested in when I wrote it.

If you have visited the CSS Zen Garden http://www.csszengarden.com website, you will be well aware of the transforming power of applying alternative style sheets to web content. If you have never visited CSS Zen Garden, I recommend you surf over there now and have your view of what web design is about turned upside down.

By providing alternative style sheets for your own visitors you are providing a way for them to modify the presentation of your content to suit their own needs. This is not the place for an in-depth look at the technical details; you will find many of these on the web, but what I can do is give you a quick overview.

As you probably already know, you can use a style sheet to alter the presentation of content that has been 'marked up' with standard HTML, for instance, all the structures in your pages are labelled appropriately.

The rules in the style sheet can be used to alter the appearance of your tagged text: for example, to make all your main headings red and very big, or make all your text display in the Georgia font.

So how do you offer alternative style sheets to your website visitors?

When you provide a choice of external style sheets, Mozilla browsers display your alternatives in the View menu, making it easy for visitors to switch between different styles. Internet Explorer does not provide this facility, although there are ways to get around this problem .

You will find a good explanation of implementing alternative style sheets on 'A List Apart' at http://www.alistapart.com/articles/alternate/. I have attempted to summarise the main points below.

There are three types of style sheet you can link to: persistent, preferred and alternate.

Persistent

As the name suggests, the rules within this style sheet are always applied to your page content, no matter what other style sheet is active (the rules in the persistent style sheet are combined with those of the active style sheet). Here is an example of a style sheet link:

```
<link rel="stylesheet" type="text/css"
href="persist.css" >
```

Preferred

The preferred style sheet is the default style sheet, the one used when the page is first loaded. To indicate that you are providing a preferred style sheet, set the 'rel' attribute to 'stylesheet' and add a title attribute:

```
<link rel="stylesheet" type="text/css"
href="pref.css" title="first alternative" >
```

Alternate

Alternative style sheets can be chosen by the visitors to your site. Set the 'rel' attribute to 'alternative stylesheet' and add a title attribute:

```
<link rel="alternate stylesheet"
type="text/css" href="alt.css" title="another
style" />
```

Each of the above style sheets could, for example, enable a visitor to change the colour of the background, or alter the size of the text, making the site more accessible to a person with a visual impairment, or someone who has dyslexia.

This tip may not be the simplest one I have ever put together, but I hope it will at least give you a sense of what is possible by using standard markup and Cascading Style Sheets.

Links

CSS Zen Garden: http://www.csszengarden.com

Making Connections Unit news: a turbo-charged sheet switcher: http://www.mcu.org.uk

Javascript style sheet switcher: http://www.alistapart.com/articles/alternate/

PHP style sheet switcher: http://www.alistapart.com/articles/phpswitch/

W3C background information: http://www.w3.org/Style/CSS/

31.

Check colour contrast by creating a greyscale image of your web page

This very simple tip will help you to check whether the colours you have chosen for your web pages have adequate contrast.

Take a screen shot of one of your web pages and open it up in an image editing program for example, Photoshop. Desaturate the image to remove all colour so that you end up with a greyscale image.

Viewing the page as a set of contrasting grey areas makes it much easier to see whether, for example, there is sufficient contrast between the background colour and text. I was reminded of this tip while reading the Techdis article 'Colour & Contrast Accessibility Issues: for the design of e-learning materials' by EA Draffan and Peter Rainger.

Links

Colour & Contrast Accessibility Issues: for the design of e-learning materials by EA Draffan and Peter Rainger:
http://www.techdis.ac.uk/seven/papers/colour-contrast5.html

32.

Make HTML pages created from MS Word more accessible

Many HTML pages are still being created using Word's in-built 'Export to HTML' function, so in this tip I explore some simple ways to make the resulting web pages a little more accessible than they would otherwise be.

Using Word to create HTML pages is not ideal, as the program has a tendency to add a lot of extra 'junk' to the resulting markup. The extra markup is used to try to make the Web page look similar to the original Word document.

However, here are two important techniques that will help to ensure your resulting web pages will be a bit more accessible, particularly for people who are using screen readers.

Use the styles facility within Word to add structure to your documents; for instance, instead of just making your headings bold, use styles to assign the appropriate level of heading. The structure will be retained when the document is converted to HTML. Screen readers will use the document structure to help make reading the web page more efficient, for example, by presenting all of the headings on a page in a summary list, so that the users can jump straight to the part they are interested in.

Add alternative text to all your images (right click and select format picture). These labels will be retained after the document is converted to HTML and can be read out to the user by screen reading software.

33.

Use the free Waizilla accessibility checker

You may, or may not, be aware that a free cross-platform website accessibility testing tool called WaiZilla, is currently being developed by Tim Roberts and a group of other programmers.

This is an Open Source project, so you can keep up with developments by visiting the website and, if you are interested and have the talent, you can contribute to the development process.

Links

WaiZilla: http://www.waizilla.org

Tim Roberts: http://www.wiseguysonly.com/

34.

Use Acrobot to catch your acronyms and abbreviations

If you find that marking up all your acronyms has become a bit of a chore, you may be interested in a tool developed by Ian Lloyd on the Accessify website: the Acrobot - Abbreviation and Acronym Generator. This useful tool will find acronyms in your HTML, add the <acronym> tag, and the appropriate title attribute. There is also a 'favelet' provided on the site to make it even easier to pass text through to Acrobot.

Links

Acrobot - Abbreviation and Acronym Generator:
http://www.accessify.com/tools-and-wizards/acrobot/default.asp

35.

Get the Web Accessibility Toolbar for Internet Explorer

In this tip I recommend you check out a new Toolbar for Internet Explorer developed by Steven Faulkner, of the National Information and Library Service (NILS). Support for the toolbar is confined to Internet Explorer on Windows. As a Mac user, I haven't been able to try it out myself. However, Gez Lemon of the website Juicy Studio is giving it glowing reviews and I trust his judgement.

According to the blurb, 'It is designed to help the user to interrogate aspects (structure/code/content) of an html document that can have an effect on the accessibility of that html document'.

It does all sorts of things I would find useful as a developer of accessible websites (validation, screen resolution changes, CSS on/off, links to online checking tools and so on), so I think you will find it very useful. You can find installation instructions and a full feature list for the accessibility toolbar on the website.

The web developer tool for Firefox is also worth checking out: http://www.chrispederick.com/work/firefox/webdeveloper/ - and is, according to Mike Pepper, 'bloody good'.

Links

Web Accessibility Toolbar by Steven Faulkner:
http://www.nils.org.au/ais/web/resources/toolbar/

The web Developer extension for Mozilla Firefox:
http://www.chrispederick.com/work/firefox/webdeveloper/

36.

Adding tags to PDF documents improves accessibility

A screen reader is not a particularly useful tool if it cannot read out the text of a document in the correct order, or if it cannot distinguish between structural elements such as headings, links or paragraph text.

With this in mind Adobe has adopted a strategy of 'marking up' the structure of PDF documents using tags, much in the same way tags are used to markup HTML pages.

Marking up the PDF document enables compatible screen readers to read the text in the appropriate order (for example, the order of the tags is the reading order of the document). This makes use of the information provided about document structure in a way that helps increase accessibility for users.

For example, in a tagged PDF document where the text is presented in columns, the screen reader understands that it should read down the first column, before moving across to read down the next column. In an untagged PDF document, it would be read from left to right across the page, which makes no sense at all when dealing with columns of text.

So how do you add tags to your PDF documents?

There are a few ways you can add tags to a PDF document. Probably the best way is to ensure that they are created automatically when converting your source document. In Word 2000 and above, do the following:

If you are using Acrobat 6, locate the 'Adobe PDF' menu and choose 'Change Conversion Settings'. In the application Settings tab, select the option to 'Enable accessibility and reflow with Tagged PDF' and click OK.

If you are using Acrobat 5, locate the 'Acrobat' menu and choose 'Change Conversion Settings'. In the 'Office' tab select the option 'Embed Tags in PDF (Accessibility, Reflow)', and click OK.

When you click the convert to PDF button, the resulting document will be a tagged document.

The above instructions assume you have installed Office 2000 or above first, and then have installed Acrobat 5 or 6.

There is a lot more to creating accessible PDF documents than just ensuring that you add tags to them. A good place to start your learning is the Adobe accessibility website. You might also want to check out my ebook, 'How to Create Accessible PDFs with Adobe Acrobat 6' available at http://www.scotconnect.com/pdfs/accesspdfs.php

Links

Ebook: How to Create Accessible PDFs with Adobe Acrobat 6:
http://www.scotconnect.com/pdfs/accesspdfs.php

Adobe Accessibility:
http://www.adobe.com/enterprise/accessibility/main.html

37.

Use Javascript to add default text to input fields

For as long as I can remember I've puzzled over whether or not to put default characters in edit boxes and text areas in my web forms. On the one hand if I don't my page will not pass Guideline 10.4, and will have no chance of WAI AAA compliance.

Guideline 10.4 exists to ensure visitors using some older screen readers (which don't recognise empty form fields) can fill in web forms.

Unfortunately, if I add default text in my form fields I create problems for another set of users, that is, those who have to delete my text before entering their own. I also create additional work for my forms-processing script, which has to check for and remove any remaining default characters. Many people don't bother deleting the default characters when adding their own text.

I have gone through periods of not adding default text and having to explain why my forms don't pass AAA web accessibility tests. I have added text and dealt with the associated problems. I had resigned myself to the thought that this was one of those web accessibility problems that has no simple solution.

However, it looks as if I may have been too quick to give up. While surfing on the Juicy Studio website, I notice that Gez Lemon (the owner of the site) was using Javascript to add default text to his forms and that the text disappeared when I clicked in the form field. The form passed the 10.4 Guideline, and caused no problems either for users or my form-processing script. The surprising thing was that it was very easy to add this facility to my own forms.

Here is an example from a field in my comments form (only the relevant attributes are shown).

```
<input type = "text" name = "membername"
value = "Name"
onfocus="if(this.value=='Name')this.value=''"
>
```

The value of the field is set to 'Name'. The inline Javascript code 'says' if there is focus on the form field (for example, I have clicked so my cursor is in the field), check the default value and if it is 'Name' make it an empty string. The relevant short script is as follows:

```
onfocus="if(this.value=='Name')this.value=''"
```

Fantastic - one more accessibility compliance problem solved. Get back to me if you are aware of any issues with this technique that I have failed to appreciate.

From the WAI Guidelines:

10.4 Until user agents handle empty controls correctly, include default, place-holding characters in edit boxes and text areas. [Priority 3] For example, in HTML, do this for TEXTAREA and INPUT.

Update to tip 37. The general consensus was that the Guideline itself is obsolete, and creates more of a usability issue than it solves.

Patrick H. Lauke has spoken to Shawn Lawton Henry, and it looks as though we will see this checkpoint disappear in the next version of the guidelines.

Gez Lemon wrote to suggest a modification of the Javascript: Rather than specifying a string literal for the check, you could reuse the same event handler with:

```
onfocus="if(this.value==this.defaultValue)this.
value=''"
```

Links

Web Content Accessibility Guidelines 1.0:
http://www.w3.org/TR/WCAG10/

Juicy Studio: http://www.juicystudio.com/

W3C Web Accessibility Initiative (WAI) Outreach Coordinator, Shawn
Lawton Henry: http://www.w3.org/People/Shawn/

Patrick H. Lauke technique:
http://www.sitepoint.com/forums/showpost.php?postid=815298&post
count=18

Tomas Caspers: http://www.einfachfueralle.de/kontakt

38.

Download ready-made style sheets to meet your access needs

I came across this tip while reading through a copy of the E-Access Bulletin: technology news for people with vision impairment.

It is a little known fact that users of Internet Explorer on Windows can apply their own style sheets to web pages by setting the appropriate accessibility option in their browser. However, the flaw in this scheme is that most users don't know how to create their own style sheets. Even if they did, it would take a while to develop one that meets their needs exactly.

Daljit Singh has addressed this problem by providing a service where users can choose their preferred font sizes and colours, and have a style sheet created for them based on those preferences. The resulting style sheet can then be downloaded, installed and set to be automatically applied to any standards-based web pages using style sheets for presentation.

While I am talking about style sheets, I'll take this opportunity to remind you of my own PHP based turbo-charged style switcher.

Links

The E-Access Bulletin: http://www.headstar.com/eab

Daljit Singh: http://www.oneformat.com/

PHP turbo-charged style switcher:
http://www.mcu.org.uk/articles/styleswitcher.php

39.

Associate form fields explicitly with their labels

Here is a handy accessibility tip that will make filling in web forms easier for screen reader users and for people with impaired motor skills. Associate form fields with their labels by making use of the 'label' element and the 'id' attribute.

When encountering a form on a web page it is easy for sighted users to work out the expected response for each form element: it is a matter of reading the label next to the field.

However, it is not always so simple for someone using a screen reader. It may not be clear which labels are associated with which fields, particularly if the page author has used tables to layout the form.

If labels are not physically close to or clearly associated with the form element, filling in a form can be extremely difficult for users of screen reading software.

There is a way to explicitly connect labels to their form elements. Each label can be identified with a name and then associated with the appropriate control using the 'id' attribute:

```
<label for="name">Name</label>
<input name=" Name" type="text" id ="name">
```

The value of the *for* attribute can be any text you choose, as long as the appropriate 'id' attribute has the same text. Using this technique provides a bonus for people with impaired motor skills because it increases the 'target area' when assigning focus to the field, for example, clicking the label or the field itself will focus the cursor in the text field or check the box if it is a radio button.

Layout your forms using CSS instead of tables

I am a fan of using CSS for layout and presentation of web pages but I do still have a few 'blind spots' when it comes to putting my good intentions into practice. For example, I still tend to use tables when creating layout for forms.

I was alerted to this tip by Tavis Reddick, the Webmaster at Fife College. While communicating about another forms-related issue, he pointed me to a useful article about using CSS to layout forms. The part about forms layout is towards the end of the article.

I won't reproduce the example code here because it is not the simplest technique I have come across. I couldn't figure out a way to simplify it for 'tip size' consumption but I thought it was worth highlighting this example. It demonstrates that CSS is flexible enough to be used for tasks beyond the simple two- or three-column page layout.

Links

Fife College: http://www.fife.ac.uk/

Practical CSS Layout Tips, Tricks, & Techniques:
http://www.alistapart.com/articles/practicalcss/

41. Web accessibility for deaf people - adding captions or providing transcripts isn't always enough

If you search the web for information related to web accessibility for deaf people, you will find plenty of advice about captioning or providing transcripts for web based audio and video material. What you are unlikely to find is much discussion related to accessibility and language. For many deaf people English is not their first language, Sign Language is.

Although Sign Language provides an equivalent for everything that can be spoken or written, for some deaf people understanding written English is a process of interpreting from English to their first language, that is, Sign Language.

Writing simple language and short sentences can help to make information more accessible to Sign Language users. However, having discussed the issues with various informed users in the past (for example, those at the Sign Language Interpreter Service in Glasgow) I believe that the most effective way to make content accessible to Sign Language users is to provide a Sign Language version of all content.

The problem here is that the obvious way to do this, that is, providing video of Sign Language interpreters, is an expensive and resource-hungry exercise. For this reason, many people are experimenting with signing avatars (virtual humans) as a way to deliver the Sign Language equivalent to written content.

Links

Sign Language Interpreter Service: http://www.slis.org.uk/

Signing Avatar from 3D.com: http://www.vcom3d.com/

Signingbooks.org:
http://www.signingbooks.org/animations/sign_language_animations.ht
m

BBC article on signing avatars:
http://www.bbcworld.com/content/clickonline_archive_35_2002.asp?p
ageid=666&co_pageid=3

42.

Don't rely on automated tools for checking web accessibility

The Disability Rights Commission (DRC) released a report in 2004 highlighting the poor accessibility of UK public websites. Among other things, the report highlighted issues related to accessibility testing:

'It is very significant that the majority of those Checkpoints that this investigation found to be the most important are qualitative, in the sense that they require the exercise of human judgement. Automatic testing tools alone cannot, therefore, verify effective compliance.'
http://www.drc-gb.org/publicationsandreports/2.pdf

Of course this is not a revelation. Web accessibility experts have been saying this for some time, echoing the line taken by the World Wide Web Consortium (W3C). In the article, 'Evaluating Web Sites for Accessibility', you will find the following statement:

'No single evaluation tool yet provides comprehensive information or captures all problems with regard to the accessibility of a site; therefore evaluation involves a combination of approaches.'
http://www.w3.org/WAI/eval/

Your site will be accessible to a wider audience if you take a comprehensive approach, and use testing by people with different abilities and skills, and evaluation by individuals with knowledge related to accessible web design.

Links

Automated testing - How useful is it? An article by Grant Broome:
http://www.gawds.org/show.php?contentid=147

43.

Don't use the statistics defence as a reason to exclude people from your content

I was recently involved in a discussion about whether website designers should be expected to accommodate Netscape 4 users.

The case against accommodating Netscape 4 users is invariably backed up with statistics about how few people now use this, admittedly flawed, browser. I've heard 'the statistics defence' (as I will call it) so often over the years that this latest evocation prompted me to think about why I don't agree with this approach.

My thoughts and arguments against the statistics defence are not yet fully formed. I would welcome any feedback on the subject. It is such a common argument against accessible web design in general, that a page containing counter-arguments would be a good resource for web accessibility advocates.

Examples of the 'statistics defence':

'We design for 17" screens because that's what most people use these days'

'We assume 92dpi resolutions because most people use a PC'

'We use IE 5 as a baseline because very few people use old browsers now'

'We don't provide an alternative to our flash site, because everyone has the flash plugin these days'

'We don't need to make our site accessible because it isn't aimed at, and doesn't get used by, disabled people'

'We design our site to work on 600 * 800 because that's what most people use'.

My arguments against this approach

I'll give my conclusion first: content on web pages needs to be accessible to Netscape 4 users and all the other user agents accessing web content. The argument that we can ignore a particular set of users because they only make up a small percentage of our audience (for instance, they use a particular browser or a particular bit of access technology) isn't one web designers should be buying into. It is irrelevant whether a person is using Netscape 4, a screen reader, or a keyboard-driven text-only browser, the issues are basically the same: it is about accessibility of web content.

The statistics defence assumes users' needs and user agents are predictable

What assumptions do many web designers make about their intended audience, for example, what browsers do they assume they are using? What screen size? screen resolutions, bandwidth, colour palette? Are those assumptions based on the computer they have on their own desk, that is, the one they are using to design the website? Probably, but is this a good approach? Probably not.

Have any of the following things changed in the past: browsers, hardware devices connected to the web, screen size, screen resolution, Markup versions? Will these things change in the future? Yes - all of them. Designing for a specific configuration of hardware and software isn't a good way of making pages future-proof. Even users with the same hardware and software resize their browser windows to suit their own preferences.

A vital lesson to learn is: change is the norm. The most predictable thing we can say is that everything changes. The best chance we have of dealing with this unpredictability is:

- Use standards so that sites have the best chance of working on the widest range of user agents.

- Create sites that are flexible enough to deliver our content - no matter what the end user is using.

That is not to say that the presentation will be the same on every device - it won't be. The presentation is important but if the content isn't accessible the presentation doesn't matter because there is nothing to present.

The web isn't paper

Cross-platform/cross-browser compatibility is the strength of the web - that was the problem it was designed to solve. Designing a web page is not like designing an advert, bus shelter notice, magazine page or document to be printed on a sheet of A4, where the amount of 'real estate', colours, text size and so on are predictable.

To take the specific issue of access for disabled people; do we have to accommodate the needs of disabled people? Do we have perfect knowledge about their access needs? The answer to the first question is yes. In the UK, the Disability Discrimination Act tells us that we can't discriminate against disabled people. The answer to the second question is no; we don't have perfect knowledge about the access needs of disabled people.

10% - 20% of people in most populations have some kind of impairment. Some of those impairments are not obvious: 8% of men have colour blindness (0.4% women), approximately 5% of the population have visual impairments - and15% dyslexia. Once people get older their eyesight, hearing and motor skills start to deteriorate

In the university where I used to work we had many disabled students. Not all of them were registered as disabled, but approximately 500 were.

Impairment	Approximate Numbers
Dyslexia	230
Blind/partially sighted	24
Deaf/partial hearing	25
Wheelchair/mobility	21
Autistic or Asperger	2
Mental health	10
Unseen disability (Epilepsy, Diabetes,etc)	91
Disability not listed	101
Two or more of the above	21

We don't have perfect knowledge about the access needs of each individual listed above - so we need general strategies to deal with this unpredictability. Dealing with the diverse needs of disabled students isn't much different from dealing with the problem of making sites work on different browsers and different hardware platforms.

We have to assume that we don't know what the end users will be using - or what their access requirements will be - and think about what this means when we make design decisions. If it turns out that our content isn't accessible on a particular browser we need to find a workaround to solve the issue while maintaining standard markup and accessible design.

We have to make our websites accessible because it is the law (in many countries).

In the UK we have the Disability Discrimination Act and the Special Needs and Disability Rights Act. In a university that means we can't discriminate against students on the grounds of their impairment; reasonable adjustment and anticipation of students' needs is required.

We can't argue that we won't accommodate disabled students because they only make up a small percentage of the student population. Equally, we shouldn't argue that we won't accommodate users with particular browsers because they are part of a minority. In relation to the particular case of Netscape 4, it is legitimate to ask users to upgrade so that they get both the content and good design - but not legitimate to argue that they won't get the content if they don't upgrade.

When a link falls at the end of a sentence always put the full stop outside the anchor tag

Consider the World Wide Web Consortium Web Content Accessibility Guidelines (WCAG), Checkpoint 10.5:

'Until user agents (including assistive technologies) render adjacent links distinctly, include non-link, printable characters (surrounded by spaces) between adjacent links.'

Generally when trying to ensure that web pages meet this particular requirement I'm thinking about navigation bars. I'm either marking them up as lists, or putting printable characters between adjacent links and, if necessary, I make them invisible via CSS.

Unfortunately, that isn't always enough to ensure a clean bill of health with regard to this particular checkpoint. It is easy, particularly on a page that gets updated often, to violate this checkpoint, for example, when a sentence that ends with a link is followed by one that begins with a link.

The solution is to get into the habit of adding the full stop after the anchor tag. As web accessibility tips go it's not the most significant one I've ever published. However, having adjacent links without a printable character between them means your well-crafted page won't pass WCAG Priority 1 and someone is bound to get in touch to alert you to that fact.

Links

WCAG Checkpoint 10.5: http://www.w3.org/TR/WCAG10/wai-pageauth.html#tech-divide-links

45.

Start with the assumption that you cannot predict the access needs of your audience

For example, a person with dyslexia may need a particular combination of text and background colours to comfortably read text on a web page. You could contact a person with this particular impairment and ask them about their preferred colours; but do all people with dyslexia have the same access needs? Unfortunately, from a web designer's point of view, the answer is no.

A better approach is to design pages so that the presentation of content can be changed by the end user. In the case of the above example, ensure that each person can change the colours to suit their own needs (for example, via browser preferences or a style switcher).

This approach can be applied to all presentation aspects, whether it be text size, layout or the choice to leave graphics on or off.

How to get XHTML pages to validate when using the blockquote tag

This is a tip for those on the bleeding edge of web page markup, that is, those marking up their web pages using XHTML strict. If you are the sort of person who uses XHTML, it is likely that you will want to ensure your pages validate when tested with the World Wide Web Consortium's markup validator.

Would it surprise you if I said the following code doesn't validate:

```
<blockquote cite="http//mywebsite.com">
Blah, blah, blah, blah.
</blockquote>
```

It looks simple enough - what could be wrong with that? I came across this very problem and spent a half an hour trying to figure out why it didn't validate. I investigated various options, including thinking that I must have some strange, invisible characters in my quoted text somewhere. After scratching my head for a while I looked at the specifications for XHTML and found the answer.

To validate as strict XHTML, you must add a block-level element around the text within the <blockquote> tag, like this:

```
<blockquote cite="http//mywebsite.com">
<p>Blah, blah, blah and so on..</p>
</blockquote>
```

Problem solved. Now my page validates and so will yours the next time you use the blockquote tag in your XHTML documents.

What is the object element for? And what's it got to do with accessibility?

Currently we add images to our pages using the img element and fancy bits of video or flash using the applet element. So why do we need the object element?

The object element was introduced as part of HTML 4, and it is designed to be used for all instances when a generic object - such as a flash movie, video or image – needs to be embedded into a web page.

That's all very well but what's it got to do with accessibility? The fantastic thing about the object elements is that you can use it to provide lots of alternative presentations of your content. You are not confined to providing a simple text equivalent as you are when using the img tag.

For example, you want to provide a Quicktime video, but it turns out that some browsers don't have the support for Quicktime. You can specify that an mpeg movie, or some other alternative format, be played instead. If the mpeg movie isn't supported you can specify that a text transcription should be used, and so on.

For browsers that don't support the object element you can provide the embed element within the object element as yet another alternative method of delivering your multi-media.

Links

W3 Schools: http://www.w3schools.com/media/media_object.asp

Juicy Studio: http://www.juicystudio.com/tutorial/html/object.asp

48.

How to hide a flash movie from screen readers and keyboard users

Adding a Flash movie to your web page may be making the content of that page inaccessible to some visitors. For example, keyboard users and people using screen readers are likely to run into the following problems:

The keyboard cannot be used to 'focus' on the flash movie, that is, the user can't tab to the movie object and explore the content.

When navigating the flash movie via the keyboard it is impossible to get back out again, making it extremely difficult to explore the rest of the page.

Here are a couple of tips for getting around the problems.

Make the Flash movie invisible to keyboard users.

If the flash movie does not contain valuable content or is for decoration, the following technique can be used to make the flash movie invisible to keyboard users and screen readers:

Use the wmode option within the embed and the object tag,

```
<object .....>
<param name="wmode" value="opaque">
<embed wmode="opaque ....>
</embed>
</object>
```

Rather than embedding the flash movie within the HTML page, create a separate HTML page that contains the movie, and link to it. This allows the users to use the back button on their browser to exit from the movie when they are finished.

Links

These tips come from an excellent article about creating accessible flash on the WebAIM website: http://www.webaim.org/techniques/flash/

49.

How to make server-side image maps accessible

Although client-side images are preferred over server-side image maps (as equivalent text can be provided for each image map 'hot-spot'), server-side image maps are sometimes necessary. For example, a server-side image can be used when the active regions of a client-side image map cannot be easily defined using an available geographic shape. In such cases the answer is to provide redundant text links relating to each link provided by the server-side image map.

The following markup example is typical of the code used to reference a server-side image map:

```
<a href="/cgi-bin/mymap.map">
<img ismap src="imagemap.gif" >
</a>
```

The web pages accessed by clicking the image map in the above example would be completely hidden to someone using a screen reader or a text-only web browser, as there is no alternative way of accessing the links provided.

Here is an example of the server-side image with alt attribute added and an alternative set of links to the same content:

```
<a href="/cgi-bin/mymap.map">
<img ismap src="imagemap.gif"
alt="Alternative text links are provided at
the foot of the page.">
</a>
```

You then make the following links available at the foot of the page:

```
<p><a href="about.html">About Us</a> | <a
href="research.html">Research</a> </p>
```
The alternative-text-based links provided at the bottom of the page imply that the image map has two hot-spots, one to find information about the organisation and another for information related to research.

50.

Develop your sites for a standards-compliant browser first, then modify for IE/Win

Develop your sites for a standards-compliant browser first, and then add workarounds for Microsoft Internet Explorer on Windows (MSIE/Win).

I picked up this tip while reading through 'Throwing Tables Out the Window', by Douglas Bowman, an article about how he used CSS to re-do the layout of the Microsoft home page.

Instead of concentrating on getting your design to work in Internet Explorer (the most popular web browser on the PC), Douglas recommends that you do all your initial work and testing using a more standards-compliant browser. This approach will cut the time you have to spend creating the inevitable workarounds required once you discover that your design falls apart in every browser apart from yours.

It is easier to tweak a standards-compliant website to work in Internet Explorer than it is to fix a site optimised for IE/Win work in more standards-compliant browsers.

Links

Throwing Tables Out the Window by Douglas Bowman:
http://www.stopdesign.com/articles/throwing_tables/

51.

How to make your pages validate when they include urls with ampersands (&'s) in them

At some point you will run your web page through the W3C validator and get the error, 'unknown entity section'. This is due to the presence of ampersands (&'s) in page link urls.

The validator assumes that this is an error because it expects an ampersand to be at the beginning of an entity.

I had this very problem when creating the weblog links for my own CMS. For me the solution was simple. I just got the CMS script to turn all ampersands into their equivalent entities.

Unfortunately, it is slightly more work to manually replace all ampersands in a page, but if you want your page to validate it is a chore you will need to attend to.

For all urls in web pages that contain ampersands, replace each ampersand (&) in urls embedded within your pages with the equivalent entity &

```
http://www.mcu.org.uk/showlog.php?weblogid=74
&contentid=1
```
needs to be modified to

```
http://www.mcu.org.uk/showlog.php?weblogid=74
&amp;contentid=1
```
Another validation problem solved.

52. Use the Flash Satay method to embed flash in your pages

Use the Flash Satay method to embed flash in your pages, and support standards.

The standard way to embed flash within a web page is to use the object element. The W3C tells us that the object element is an 'all-purpose solution to generic object inclusion'. That's fine and dandy. However, the object element is not supported by all web browsers.

Developers have tried to work around this deficiency by adding the non-standard (but working) embed tag into their markup, effectively repeating all the necessary attributes in each tag. Using the embed tag means that pages will no longer validate - a situation which makes developers who pride themselves on their adherence to standards rather uncomfortable.

During a discussion about this issue on the Guild of Accessible Web Designers mailing list, I was alerted to an article by Drew McLellan, who addresses this very problem. Drew provides a solution that ensures flash works in many more browsers without failing validation tests, a solution he calls the 'Flash Satay method'.

Links

Guild of Accessible Web Designers: http://www.gawds.org/

Flash Satay Article bu Drew Mclellan:
http://www.alistapart.com/articles/flashsatay/

53.

Use a Content Management System that helps you build an accessible website

It is hard to create and manage an accessible website without a set of tools fit for the job. Luckily for us, more of those who produce web design applications and content management systems are waking up to the fact that accessible web design is here to stay.

Search Google for 'Accessible Content Management Systems' and you will find that there are now plenty to choose from. However, I am allowing myself the liberty of recommending just one CMS in this tip – because I wrote it myself. It is the CMS used by the Guild of Accessible Web Designers, built from the ground up, to help the user create accessible websites.

Users fill in browser-based forms to create and edit pages. It includes WYSIWYG (what you see is what you get) editors for those who are less keen to code by hand. The CMS is not suitable for corporate giants, but it will be work fine for individuals, businesses or small colleges.

Links

QnECMS - the accessible content management system:
http://www.qnecms.co.uk

54.

Use the simplified 'box model hack' to set consistent text sizes

I came across this great tip while reading 'Bulletproof Web Design' by Dan Cederholm – a book I recommend to you without reservation.

Absolute-size keywords are a great way to set font sizes in your web page. The options you have are:

xx-small

x-small

small

medium

large

x-large

xx-large

Here is an example of absolute-size keywords used to set the size of elements when using style sheets:

```
body
{
font-size: small;
}
```

However, there is a problem with keywords. IE5 for Windows sets text size one full step larger than other browsers: so if you set your text size using the keyword small, it will work as expected in most browsers, whereas in IE/5 Win the text will look bigger, that is, it will look as though you set it to medium.

Tantek Celik discovered the Box Model Hack to get around this problem. It is a rather complicated-looking bit of jiggery-pokery that you will find on the web by Googling for the term Box Model Hack.

In this tip I suggest the use of a much simpler-looking hack by Edwardson Tan. It gives the same results as the Box Model Hack:

```
Body {
Font-size: small;
}
* html body
{
font-size: x-small; /*for IE5/Win */
f\ont-size: small; /* for other IE versions */
}
```

The * html selector exploits a bug in IE which results in this declaration being served to IE browsers only. Of IE browsers, IE5 is the only one that ignores the property set using the backslash – so it gets text set to x-small, while the others gets text set to small.

Links

Simplified Box Model Hack:

http://www.info.com.ph/~etan/w3pantheon/style/modifiedsbmh.html

55.

HTML 4.01 is the final version of HTML and it will be around for a while yet

One of the most important steps you can take to ensure that your web pages will be accessible is to code them using standards-based markup. Coding to standards will reduce development and maintenance costs, make your content more flexible and ensure your pages will be 'future compliant'.

But which standard should you adopt? Surely the one thing we can be sure of is that standards are always changing and being 'upgraded'.

There is one standard you can rely on to never change, and that is HTML 4.01. The World Wide Web Consortium (W3C) states that - apart from fixing the bugs - HTML 4.01 is the final version of HTML.

In a sea of changing and unpredictable variables, there are few rocks for you to base the building of your site on. However, marking up the content of your site using valid HTML 4.01 is one.

So should you code your pages using HTML 4.01 or make the leap to XHTML or XML? That is up to you to decide, but consider this quote from Tim Berners-Lee, the inventor of the web and director of the W3C:

'I think HTML 4.0 will be a standard which you will be able to read in 200 years time. There is so much HTML. There is also enough investment in it that any new format will have ways of moving an HTML website into that format. But - do use standard HTML!! If you use some proprietary version then you could be stuck with material which makes no sense in 200 years time - or 20.'

Links

Tim Berner-Lee quote:

http://www.time.com/time/community/transcripts/1999/092999berners-lee.html

World Wide Web Consortium HTML 4.01 specification:

http://www.w3.org/TR/html4/

56.

Check your website design on every browser, on every operating system

There has never been a better time to create standards-compliant websites. Browser manufacturers now take standards compliance more seriously than they have in the past.

Unfortunately, there are still web browsers that interpret cascading style sheets in unpredictable and non-standard ways.

One of the best tools I have come across for checking how a website looks in different browsers is the web-based service, BrowserCam. BrowserCam displays screenshots of site designs on many different browsers – allowing problems to be identified and providing an opportunity to get them fixed before complaints from visitors highlight any issues.

The drawback of using such a service is that it is quite expensive ($500pa) – so there is a second part to this tip. You can lower the cost by grouping together with other people to raise the money for a shared BrowserCam licence. To help you organise your funding drive you can use a service called Fundable, a website set up for just this type of activity. I got my own access to BrowserCam via participation in a Fundable group licensing scheme – see the archived fundable browsercam page for inspiration: https://www.fundable.org/groupactions/browsercam.2005-09-27.8172399064.

If you can't afford a licence and can't find enough people to group with, there is an open source version of BrowserCam called Browsershots, http://browsershots.org/

Links

BrowserCam: http://www.browsercam.com/

https://www.fundable.org/

Browsershots: Open source, free service that aims to provide a similar function to browser cam: www.browsershots.org

57.

Mark up tables using the correct tags

An important step towards making data tables accessible is to use the table tags correctly, for example, th for table headings, td for cells with data in them, caption for adding a caption to the table.

When used as intended, these tags provide information about the relationship between cells within a table. This is invaluable for people using assistive technologies such as screen readers, as these tools can use the table structure to present the content in a way that makes sense to the user.

58.

Use the summary attribute to provide alternative access to table content

The summary attribute can be used to provide a verbose description of the purpose of the table, or, in the case of complex tables, a complete summary of the table contents. Employing the summary attribute to provide the content is one way to help someone who is using a voice or Braille browser and who might find the table itself difficult to interpret.

Caption tag

The caption tag can be used to connect a description of the content of a table to the table it relates to.

The following example shows the correct use of the th, td, caption and summary attributes:

Jim, Pat and John's favourite colours and pastimes

	Jim	Pat	John
Favourite colour	Green	Turquoise	Yellow
Favourite pastime	Photography	Swimming	Badminton

The HTML of the table:

```
<table summary="Example table showing Jim,
Pat and John's favourite colours and
pastimes." border="1" cellpadding="15">
```

```
<caption> Jim, Pat and John's favourite
colours and pastimes</caption>
<tr>
<th></th>
<th>Jim</th>
<th>Pat</th>
<th>John</th>
</tr>
<tr>
<th>Favourite colour</th>
<td>Green</td>
<td>Turquoise</td>
<td>yellow</td>
</tr>
<tr>
<th>Favourite pastime</th>
<td>photography</td>
<td>swimming</td>
<td>badmington</td>
</tr>
</table>
```
The summary attribute is not visible to those using standard GUI (Graphical User Interface) web browsers but can be used by assistive technologies such as screen and braille readers.

59.

Use id and header attributes to make complex tables accessible

When tables are large and complicated it can be difficult for people who use screen readers to extract useful information from them.

Access technologies such as screen readers or braille displays read the data in tables a row at a time, left to right across the page as illustrated in the following example:

1	2	3
4	5	6

In a table with many columns and many rows this can present a problem. As more rows are read, trying to remember which header matches up with which particular piece of data becomes difficult.

For example, the table below shows Cascading Style Sheet bugs in Internet Explorer 5x, compiled by CSS Pointers Group at http://css.nu/pointers/bugs.html. The original table has 13 rows - I have just extracted the first four rows for illustrative purposes.

Workarounds for CSS bugs with Internet Explorer 5x, (W=Win '95 M=Mac)

CSS Property/ Problem	Description	Workaround	Notes/Footnotes
absolute/relative positioning	absolute child loses position	set the width property of the parent element	W demo

Classes set as number (i.e. P.1)	recognised due to error-recovery	Illegal syntax; don't use	W95, NT (6)
color	f0f0f0 rendered	illegal syntax; include the required '#'	W95, NT

Try this exercise. Hide the column headers in the table above, by placing a ruler or piece of paper over them. Gradually work your way down the table reading out the contents of each cell. If you are anything like me, you will begin to feel anxious about what each cells represents. As a sighted person I can keep glancing up the column to reassure myself of the nature of the information I am reading. If I am using a screen reader or a braille display, this is not an option.

To help with this problem HTML 4 provided new attributes: id and headers.

id and headers

By giving each table heading a unique label (the 'id' attribute) and then associating each of the data cells with that label using the 'header' attribute, HTML 4 allows new web browsers to give appropriate feedback to those using assistive technologies.

For example, here is how the HTML looks for the above table using the 'id' attribute in the headers and the 'header' attribute in each of the data cells.

```
<table border="1" summary="Workarounds for CSS
bugs with Internet Explorer 5x, (W=Win '95
M=Mac)" cellpadding="10">

<caption style="font-size: 120%; font-style:
bold">Workarounds for CSS bugs with Internet
Explorer 5x, (W=Win '95 M=Mac)</caption>
```

```html
<tr>

<th id="header1">CSS Property/ Problem</TH>

<th id="header2">Description</TH>

<th id="header3">Workaround</th>

<th id="header4">Notes/Footnotes</th>

</tr>

<tr>

<td headers="header1">absolute/relative
positioning</TH>

<td headers="header2"> absolute child loses
position</td>

<td headers="header3"> set the width property of
the parent element</td>

<td headers="header4">W demo<</td>

</tr>

<tr>

<td headers="header1">Classes set as number (i.e.
P.1)</td>

<td headers="header2">recognised due to error-
recovery</td>

<td headers="header3">Illegal syntax; don't
use</td>

<td headers="header4">W95, NT (6)</td>

</tr>

<tr>

<td headers="header1">color</td>

<td headers="header2">f0f0f0 rendered</td>

<td headers="header3">illegal syntax; include the
required '#'</td>

<td headers="header4">W95,NT</td>

</tr>

<tr>

<td headers="header1">width on body is
ignored</td>
```

```
<td headers="header2"> ignored</td>
<td headers="header3">use width on DIV
instead</td>
<td headers="header4"> W95, NT</td>
</tr>
</table>
```

A screen reader will read out the first data row as follows:

CSS Property/ Problem: absolute/relative positioning,

Description: absolute child loses position,

Workaround: set the width property of the parent element,

Notes/Footnotes: W demo

And the second row:

CSS Property/ Problem: Classes set as number (i.e. P.1),

Description: recognised due to error-recovery,

Workaround: Illegal syntax; don't use,

Notes/Footnotes: W95, NT (6)

There are other techniques to make tables accessible, for example, the scope attribute can be used to associate all of the cells in a column or row. However, research by Roger Hudson published in his article 'Accessible Data Tables' suggests that the 'id', header combination is the most accessible technique.

Links

Accessible Data Tables article by Roger Hudson:
http://www.usability.com.au/resources/tables.cfm

HTML or XHTML? It's not as important as you think

Web developers spend time fretting over whether they should be using XHTML or HTML to mark up the content of their web pages. Much can be written about the pros and cons on both sides:

- HTML can be viewed as the markup language of the past. The W3C states we should always use the most up-to-date technologies.

- HTML is the only markup language you can rely on to consistently deliver your content on any browser, as it will never change in the future.

- XHTML was designed to make it easier for machines to process web pages. The content is highly structured and doesn't include information about the presentation of that content.

- XHTML is designed to be an application of XML. However, most current browsers don't understand XML (and therefore XHTML) and just treat it as 'tag soup'.

- Delivering true XHTML can crash certain browsers. If marked up incorrectly, it can deliver nothing at all - which is the ultimate in inaccessible content.

Much more can be written in relation to all of the above points but this just gives a flavour of the issues.

The good news is that, in most cases it doesn't matter whether you use HTML or XHTML. Both HTML and XHTML (in all their variants) can be used to deliver highly structured or loosely structured data. This insight came to me while I was drinking coffee in my local Costa when preparing for one of my training courses. What is more important is to decide what you are using, say what you are using, and follow the rules implied by your choice.

We could argue about whether French or English is a better language to communicate in, but we would be wasting our breath. In order to understand you if you are speaking French I need to know it is French you are speaking and I need to understand French.

The same goes for markup languages. A web browser needs to know what standard you are using and you need to adhere to the rules outlined by that standard. The web browser doesn't value XHTML above HTML or for that matter HTML 4.01 Strict above HTML 4.01 Transitional. The browser just deals with your web page according to the rules it is given; there is no value judgement involved.

So as a web developer you should fret less about what you choose to use, and concentrate on how you apply it to your web pages.

Links

Choosing a DOCTYPE: http://www.juicystudio.com/article/choosing-doctype.php

Accessibility Is Not Enough: http://www.useit.com/alertbox/accessibility.html

Visit http://www.jimbyrne.co.uk for the latest tips on creating accessible websites.

Send me an email to say hello and to tell me whether you found this book useful or not. Good luck with your quest to design accessible websites.

The End

Jim Byrne

Email: webdesign@jimbyrne.co.uk

LaVergne, TN USA
12 January 2010
169680LV00008B/53/A